Meet in the Meadow

Trudy Bangen Hofer

Cover illustration by Lerentia Basson.

National Library of Canada Cataloguing in Publication Data

Hofer, Trudy Bangen, 1967-
    Meet in the meadow / Trudy Bangen Hofer.
Includes bibliographical references.
ISBN 1-4120-0020-3
    1. Hofer, Trudy Bangen, 1967- --Childhood and youth.
2. Farm
life--Minnesota--Climax.   I. Title.
F614.C54H63 2003   977.6'95   C2003-
901270-0

TRAFFORD

This book was published *on-demand* in cooperation with Trafford Publishing.
On-demand publishing is a unique process and service of making a book available for retail sale to the public taking advantage of on-demand manufacturing and Internet marketing. **On-demand publishing** includes promotions, retail sales, manufacturing, order fulfilment, accounting and collecting royalties on behalf of the author.

Suite 6E, 2333 Government St., Victoria, B.C. V8T 4P4, CANADA
Phone   250-383-6864   Toll-free   1-888-232-4444 (Canada & US)
Fax   250-383-6804   E-mail   sales@trafford.com
Web site   www.trafford.com   TRAFFORD PUBLISHING IS A DIVISION OF TRAFFORD
HOLDINGS LTD.
Trafford Catalogue #03-0383   www.trafford.com/robots/03-0383.html

10   9   8   7   6   5   4   3   2

THIS BOOK IS DEDICATED TO

MY DAUGHTERS

JESSICA ANN MARIE

JANELLE HANNAH JEAN

JOSEY KATE LYN

TABLE OF CONTENTS

CHAPTER ONE

THE SUMMER STORM

"Only two weeks until school starts and our summer vacation will be over," Jessica said as her cousin Sonney was quickly twirling around on the big tire swing at our grandfathers farm.

"Yeah, I can't wait to see all of my friends again, but it's been nice out here, too."

The wind was really beginning to blow now. Leaves were being blown off the trees. The sun was covered with dark gray clouds, and the wind had become chilled.

As we walked up to the house, the sweet smell of warm apple crisp filled the air. As we sat down at the kitchen table, Grandma Shirley was pulling two dessert plates from the cupboard. "I bet I can guess what you two want? How about a piece of this fresh apple crisp?"

"Sure," Sonney said with a big smile on his face.

As I finished my dessert and put my plate in the sink, I thought of how great it was to stay with Grandpa and Grandma and play outside with Grandpa's collie, who we named Copper, and Grandma's cat named Kitty B, for Kitty Beautiful.

Just as we walked back outside, we heard Grandpa yelling to us from the barn. "You kids better put your bikes in the garage before that storm gets here.

Across the creek, over in the pasture, lightning had struck just as we walked out of the garage. It sure was loud. Just as if a cannon had gone off right in the yard. The lightning lit up the gloomy gray sky. The wind had picked up quite steadily now. As we walked toward the barn, we noticed the sky getting even darker. Almost black at times. Grandpa looked out of the barn and began to motion for us to come quickly.

We began to run towards the door, encouraging Copper and Kitty B to run with us. "Come quickly Jessica and Sonney. This storm

2

looks like a whopper," Grandpa said as we got to the doorway of the old red barn.

"Grandma is in the cellar and has lit a few candles. I think we better stay down there until the storm passes. It is safer down there. Let's get Copper and Kitty B to come down, too."

We walked slowly down the dust creaking stairs. The candle light was dim, but bright enough to see. As Grandpa came down the stairs, the candle light began to flicker. Almost going out.

I could hear the wind howling. Almost as if it was talking to us. Copper and Kitty B laid down on an old dusty rug in the corner, as Sonney and I sat on a large wooden crate. All if a sudden I heard a loud boom of thunder and the crash of a window breaking. I was so scared I jumped.

"Don't worry," Grandpa said, "it will be over soon."

The thunder sounded like it was getting closer and closer until it was right on top of the big red barn. The boards were creaking, the wind was howling, and the rain was hitting the windows hard. Within a few minutes the sound of the rain began to soften. The thunder was beginning to sound faint. Soon, no thunder, no rain.

"I think I'll go up and check to see if the storm has passed," Grandpa said as he smiled at us. We were still sitting on that crate with our hands together between our knees, trying to pretend we weren't scared. Just as he opened up the cellar door, the candles blew out from the big gush of cool wind. While Grandma walked up the stairs, we got up and stood at the bottom waiting for the o.k. to come up. Copper and Kitty B ran up the stairs and were glad to get out of the cellar.

"Looks like it's over," Grandpa said with a big sigh of relief.

Sonney and I looked at each other and took a deep breath and began to laugh. "I still love summer vacation," Sonney said as his leg reached for the first step, "but now we will have a good story to tell all our friends when we go back to school."

CHAPTER TWO

FINDING DARLA

"Nella," Mom yelled from outside in the yard, "did the phone ring?"

"Yes, someone named Mr. Bagley. I wrote his phone number on the notebook on the table. Who is Mr. Bagley?" I asked.

My mom just smiled and said it was a surprise. I didn't really care anyway. I walked outside and sat on the steps in front of our house. Just as I could feel my eyes swell up with tears, my mom opened the door and sat down beside me on the steps.

"I've got a very special surprise for you today, Nella."

I didn't even answer her or look at her. I didn't want her to see me crying. All of a sudden she placed the palm of her hand on my cheek and turned my head towards her.

"Why are you crying, Nella? What's wrong?" she asked.

"Today would have been Mooney's 2nd birthday. I miss him, even though he has been gone for three months. And I'm still mad at our neighbor for running over him. He was my best friend," I sobbed, with both of my hands held up to my face as the tears rolled down my cheeks and onto my fingers.

"Oh, honey, you know that it was an accident," Mom said. She wiped my tears with her fingers and hugged me.

"I know your right," I said, "but it still makes me sad. He was a good dog."

Mom looked at me, then smiled and said, "I think I know just what you need. How about you and I take a drive over to Mr. Bagley's farm and take a look at his new puppies his collie Lucy had about eight weeks ago? Would you like that?"

"No," I said angrily, "I don't want another puppy, I want Mooney."

"Well, I'm going there anyway, so you might as well ride along," she said cheerfully.

"O.K., I'll go." I didn't care about any other

puppy. I missed Mooney too much. I wished I had stayed home as we drove down Mr. Bagley's long, narrow driveway.

As we pulled up to the house, an old man with gray hair and a long white beard waved to my mom and yelled hello.

"Come with me," Mr. Bagley said slowly, "Lucy and the puppies are in the barn. We've got two puppies left. I plan to keep one for myself. So you go ahead and choose on to take home with you."

"Look how cute they are Nella. Which one do you want to take home?" Mom said as she bent down to pet them.

"I don't care!" I yelled.

Just as I said that, the bulb in the corner of the old barn, burnt out. It got really dark in the corner where the puppies were. Mr. Bagley went to get a new bulb from the workbench. But as he put it in, and the light came on, Lucy was in the corner, but with only one puppy.

"Where's the other puppy?" I asked.

"We better find her," Mom said, "soon it will be dark outside and she may get lost."

"Nella?" said Mr. Bagley, "Do you think

you can find her?"

"Well, I'll try."

I looked all over in the old rickety barn, but found nothing. I even searched behind the barn in the tall grass, taking each step slowly, in case she was hiding in there. Then I thought to myself how little she was and she was probably very scared and lonely. I looked behind the big oak tree in the middle of Mr. Bagley's yard, but no puppy. And it was getting dark now. What if I didn't find her? What would happen to her?

Holding the scrap of food Mr. Bagley me to feed her, I stomped over to the car.

"I can't find her, mom!"

Just then I felt something rub up against the back of my leg. I looked down and sure enough it was the puppy.

"Why, that little rascal," Mom said laughing.

"Mom, I think we should take her home with us," I smiled, suddenly feeling happier then when we arrived at the farm.

Mr. Bagley looked at Mom with a big grin on his face, "I'll pack some of her food in a bag for you then."

As we drove away, Mom tapped her fingers to the beat of the music on the radio. And I held the puppy in my old red sweatshirt. "I think we should name her Darla," I said smiling at my mom.

"O.K., Darla it is."

As I bent down to hug Darla, she turned and licked my nose with her wet warm tongue. I knew I had found a new friend.

CHAPTER THREE

RIVER'S EDGE

Exploring the Red River of the North was always an adventure.

As we made our way down the beaten path, the sun was gleaming. With our skin saturated with bug spray, my sister Torrey and I followed the trail of worn out grass.

Our favorite spot was easy to find. The grass was pushed down flat into the dirt on the river bank, from being used repeatedly.

As we settled in, the aroma of our father's freshly harvested wheat field, along the river, floated over on a soft gust of wind. We baited our fishing hooks and cast our rods. Then we sat there and waited. The sun warmed our skin; it was so peaceful. We sat there and watched the long narrow blades of grass swaying gently in the cool breeze. We watched the dirty grimy water rippling softly as it flowed to the north. Crisp brown and gold leaves occasionally floated down around us from the towering trees.

When we would least expect it, our rods would bow. We usually screamed to one another with excitement. Pulling the rods out of the grungy water was tricky. Most of the time, the line would get tangled in the long slimy weeds just below the surface.

Once we got the line free and clear, we were lucky to find a catfish or bullhead on the hook. Trying to grab the fish and take it off the hook felt like trying to get a hold of a bar of soap in a bathtub full of warm water.

After we threw the fish back in the river, it was time to eat. Our lunch box gave off the stench of rotten apples. The thirst quenching flavor of diluted lemonade hit the back of our parched throats, as we sipped our drinks. Once our thirst had been satisfied, we would relish the flavor of our sandwiches made with crunchy peanut butter. The cool lemonade would wash our mouths, and prepare it for the smooth taste of our milk chocolate candy bars that would follow. The odor of fish and mud on our hands didn't even bother us.

Now and then, an old rotting log would come into view, floating silently northward. We would persuade each other into imagining it could be a crocodile working his way towards us. But within seconds, we would turn to each other and laugh.

In a moment of tranquility, you could hear the gentle ripples of water and the calling back and forth of several different species of birds. The chirping of crickets and grasshoppers was intense. Sometimes the volume of it all, while we sat there in silence, was like watching a big screen television with stereo surround sound.

By the end of the day, the sunlight flickered between the branches of the trees. The potency of bug spray had long worn off. As I used the palm of my hands to boost me up, the once cool and firm ground beneath me, was warm and indented.

Torrey glanced my way and asked, "Got plans for tomorrow?"

I just smiled lazily.

CHAPTER 4

LUCKY DOG

It's really windy out today, Megan thought to herself. I hope I don't have any trouble crossing. That boat is so small. But it has enough room to carry me and my dog back home. Megan missed Lucky. But she was sure Grandpa took good care of him. He thought it was better for him to be on the other side of the creek. Megan looked out at the farm. Everything was flooded.

Megan stood by the edge of the water, biting her bottom lip. She wondered how long it would be before she would get everything into the boat and make it across the creek, where the road was flooded.

Before long all was ready in the small fishing boat. Megan put her bags in first. Then came to new window, which would replace the she had at home in her bedroom that had gotten broken by her baseball. She was now ready. All she had left to grab was her dog, Lucky.

The wind gusts were strong, and it started to rain. Just as Megan went to step into the boat, carrying Lucky, she slipped. "Lucky," she screamed as she dropped into the cold water.

"Lucky. Lucky. Oh no. What should I do? I don't know how to swim!"

The current swept Lucky up the creek. Megan got back into the boat and started the small engine. She drove quickly down the creek after Lucky. The wind and rain made it difficult for her to steer the boat in a steady direction.

As the wind kept pushing the water and Lucky northward, one thing was on Megan's mind. The opening. There, the creek runs into the Red River of the North. What if they were pushed into the opening? They'd be pulled under the water by the current.

The boat headed north. The water was so high. The tree line between the creek bank and field was flooded. Trees were uprooted and floating in the rushing creek water.

Before long, they were only one half of a mile away from the opening. The rain had made everything wet and muddy. Megan could see and hear the water churning and twirling at the river's opening. Megan's heart was beating as if she were pounding on a drum.

"Where's Lucky?" she cried. "I can't see him anymore."

As Megan made her way further upstream, she yelled, "There you are. I found you."

Lucky had managed to paddle his way to a big tree close to the creek's bank. Megan made her way to the tree. She threw a rope around a tree branch. She tied the other end to the boat.

Megan struggled as she pulled, but the rope was slippery from the rain. She managed to reach Lucky and get him into the boat. Then a huge gust a wind came along. That, combined with the mighty current of the water rocking the boat, made Megan topple back, still holding Lucky. The window fell out and shattered on a tree that lay next to the creek bank.

Startled by the shattering sound, Megan let go of the rope. Then the rope came loose from the tree branch. The boat began to proceed towards the river. As Megan tried to grab the rope, the mud and rain made it too slimy to grasp onto.

The sound of the opening was now like standing next to Hoover Dam. Lucky was barking loudly.

As Megan tried to steer the boat towards the creek bank, she saw several large trees just ahead. She began to yell. But it happened too quickly. The boat hit the trees like a head on collision. Megan and Lucky fell out of the boat. She grabbed onto his collar tightly as she clutched onto one of the trees that lay partially in the field. She pulled herself and Lucky to the creek bank.

Megan watched as the small boat entered the opening. It was being bounced around like a rubber ball. Soon it was gone. The water continued to churn. Trees and branches from downstream were being fed into the opening.

Megan hugged her dog. "Are you o.k.?" Megan said sobbing. As she held him tightly, she said, "Well, I'm all right. Let's go home. You know, your one lucky dog!"

Megan just smiled at him as she began to walk towards the farm.

CHAPTER FIVE

WHO IS MITCHELL?

"I want my football," he said as he got out of the car.

"O.K. Mitchell," his mother said. She handed him the ball.

His smile was friendly; especially with his one front tooth missing. His skin was pale. His hair was short and blonde. In the sun it looked almost white. He looked about eight years old, but his wire frame glasses made him look older.

He strolled over to the playground. His blue polo shirt looked new. He was in style with his baggy blue jean shorts and black tennis shoes. He glided over to the monkey bars. His tall slim frame made it easy for him to sway back and forth. He moved from one side to the other quickly.

"Do you want to play catch?' he asked a

small girl with a blonde ponytail.

"My name is Josey," the girl said while giggling at him. "I don't know how," she said. Mitchell handed her the ball.

"Oops, hold the ball like this," he said. He placed her fingers on the white laces of the football. She gave it a throw and ran away laughing.

He slowly walked over to the picnic table where is mother and baby sister were sitting. He just stood there, biting on his thin bottom lip. Then he raised his eyebrows while tossing his ball from one hand to the other.

"Why don't you ask your sister to play?" his mother asked.

"Megan just wants to play on the slides with the other girls anyway."

After he took a long deep breath, he began kicking the ball up onto the air. Hoping to entice the other kids into playing with him. But they continued screaming and laughing to each other, as if they didn't notice him.

The day was cloudy, cool, and breezy. You could smell the freshly cut grass surrounding the playground. There were three bright yellow slides on a faded wooden structure. There were two sets of swings and a lot of sand. Several picnic tables surrounded the park.

"Hey Megan, "he yelled, "There's a baby rabbit over there. Come and see."

Soon all the other kids had gone. All but one little girl, Josey. She was the girl he tried to teach to throw the football. He ran over to her by the swing and politely offered to push her.

"No, I want to do it by myself," she said as she climbed onto the low swing.

As he lowered himself carefully to hang from the monkey bars, his shirt fell down to his neck. Megan and Josey giggled as they watched him. They jumped on the tire swing and asked Mitchell to join them. They twirled around fast, with his end of the tire swing almost touching the sand.

"Hey, that was fun," he yelled as the girls ran away and left him alone.

Soon after that, his mother yelled to him, "Mitchell and Megan, it's time to go home. Marley needs to take her afternoon nap.

He grabbed his football from the sand, with a frown on his face, and shuffled his feet as he walked to the car.

19

CHAPTER SIX

MITCHELL II

I don't know why I bring my football with me every time I come to this playground. There is never anyone here that I know. That girl Josey would play with me, but she's too little. She's only three years old she told me.

Mom told me to ask Megan to play with me, but she only wants to play with other girls. You would think she likes football. She always watches it on television with me and Dad on sundays. I have two sisters, and they are no fun at all. Marley is only nine months old, so I guess she's too small to play stuff like that right now.

Next time we come here I will leave my football at home. I can play on the tire swing again. The girls like to laugh and scream when I push them around really fast. The slides are o.k. too.

I'm almost too big for these monkey bars. I'm tall enough that when I hang upside down, I can almost touch the sand with my fingertips. The monkey bars at my school are much higher. I like those better anyway. I don't know why we can't go over there and play. Mom says this park is always nice and clean. And not too crowded. I guess she has a point.

I wonder why the other boys here don't have a football. Don't they like football? Maybe they don't know anything about the game. No, that's crazy. Who doesn't know about football? I would ask them to play, but I don't know any of them. But if I did ask them to play and they agreed, we would have a lot of fun. What if they didn't know anything about football, and I had to teach them everything I know about the game. I know a lot about football. I could be their coach. Wow! That would be really cool.

And I never should have yelled so loud when I saw that baby rabbit. All those kids ran over there and scared it away. I knew it was no use for me to go over there. It would have been gone already. Rabbits move pretty fast.

Well, I'm too shy to ask those other boys to play. But I'd never tell my sister Megan that. She'd just laugh at me and call me a scaredy cat. That would really make me mad. I'll tell her I just wanted to play with her and the other girls on the tire swing. She would believe me. She believes everything I tell her. Like that time last summer when I told her I took her wad of bubble gum off her dinner plate and dropped it in her pop can. I really threw it in the grass. Then I put my pet earthworm, Sidney, in the can. She drank all her pop. She didn't even know what I did. She still doesn't. Boy, if she did, she would throw a big fit, like a baby. She'd probably start crying, too. Mom would ground me for the rest of my life! I guess I better not ever tell her about that one.

Maybe next weekend I'll call Sonney. He's my favorite cousin. He knows all about football and golf. Yeah, that's a good idea!

CHAPTER SEVEN

MICE MANIA

Have you ever wondered why there are so many mice in the world?

They breed at a fast rate. This ensures that they will survive. A female house mouse starts to breed when she is only six weeks old. She can have up to ten litters in a year. This means she can give birth up to ten times a year and have five to seven babies each time. Just imagine that! If all the young survive, one pair of mice could become half a million mice in just one year. Wow! That's a lot of mice.

Before mice are born, the mother has built a cozy nest of woven grass, straw, and plant pieces. A house mouse may use bits of shredded paper and cloth. They make their nests in a safe place, such as under the floorboards or behind a wall. Around twenty days after mating, the mother gives birth. That's really quick. The babies don't look like mice. They are pink and have no hair at all. They also have no ears and are blind.

After two days their tails begin to grow longer. Their eyes are more easy to see. When four days old, they will make ultrasonic squeaks. The squeaks are too high to be heard by the human ear. Their mother can hear them though.

The mouse is a good mother. If any babies wiggle out of the nest they will squeak. Using her mouth, she will carry them back to safety. Mice are small defenseless mammals. Because of this, they are easy prey for other creatures.

The mother mouse feeds her young milk on a regular basis. Several times a day they will nurse and drink milk. This gives them the energy they need to grow. And they grow at an amazing rate, They will be weaned at about eighteen days old. This means they will no longer be able to drink their mothers milk. That doesn't seem long, does it? Once off mothers milk, they are given seeds and grain.

Once weaned, the mice become curious

about their surroundings. They leave the nest for short periods of time. Soon they will be ready to go out on their own to look for food. When they do, they have many problems to face. Such as lack of food and predators. And as they themselves begin to breed, there is over crowding. Many mice move on to a new area.

Their survival depends on their ability to find food and a new home as soon as possible.

It's easy to see why we have such a massive supply of mice in the world.

The next time you see a mouse, just think of how many brothers and sisters it has.

CHAPTER EIGHT

ENDANGERED

Have you ever thought of people as dangerous? Now that's a question that really makes you think about the human race, uh?

People have been called the most dangerous animals of all. You are probably wondering why. Well, take the following into consideration. They threaten animals and environments everywhere. Read on to find out how.

The first North Americans wiped out Wooly Mammoths and Giant Ground Sloths. European explorers exterminated Sea Cows and Elephant Birds.

Between 1970 and 1993, poachers in Africa slaughtered more than 60,000 Black Rhinoceroses. They have been hunted for their horns for centuries. This animal is now on the verge of extinction. The word extinct means no longer living. When the last living member of a species dies, the species is extinct.

The ban called "Ivory of Flames," in Kenya, burned the tusks of 1,000 elephants in support for banning the ivory trade. Ivory prices and the poaching of elephants have now declined as a result.

The popular Skin Trade is also an interesting issue. The beautiful fur of the spotted cat has tempted many hunters. Declining the number of some large cat species dramatically. In the 1970's, most countries agreed to stop the trade in skins of endangered cats. Any support is better than none at all.

What about the cute and cuddly Koala Bears? They are not usually afraid of people. In the past they were an easy target for hunters who wanted their fur. Two million skins were exported from Australia in 1924. Soon after this, it became illegal to hunt them.

Then we have our Fatal Fashion problem. Crocodiles, Alligators, Snakes and Lizards are killed on a regular basis. They are killed to make leather boots, belts and purses. Many of these reptiles are now endangered as a result.

What do you know about the Bald Eagle? In 1963, about 400 breeding pairs were left in the United States. An effort to save them, about 30 years long, has proven to be very successful. The effort included protecting their habitat, banning the insecticide DDT and hunting. Now the number of breeding pairs has grown to more than 4,000. Wow, what a great number, uh? No longer is the Bald Eagle on the endangered species list. Now that's progress.

The Rainforest is also in danger. A rainforest is a tropical forest that receives at least 100 inches of rain each year, with little differences in temperature. Each year, people burn huge areas of the forest. And species species of animals and plants become extinct. More than 15,000. That number is catastrophic when you think about it. All the rainforests will be completely destroyed in the next 30 years if this does not stop.

Whenever people move into new habitats, other animals are forced to move out. By one means or another. It all continues as the growth of the human population invades our last wild wildernesses.

These are all startling facts. They really make a person think about why this has to happen. Unfortunately, as people and time move forward, we will continue to see these problems. But with peoples efforts, hopefully some of it can be slowed down. Maybe even stopped. It would really be worth it. Don't you think so, too?

In this book, chapter 8, which is entitled "ENDANGERED", is a very brief piece filled with exciting facts. Hopefully interesting enough to make you want to read more about one or more of the topics mentioned. Reading can open many doors for you. So, the next time you find yourself with nothing to do, just settle into your favorite spot and grab a good book and enjoy!

SOURCES

Eyewitness Books. *Mammal.* New York: Alfred A. Knopf, 1989.

Seidensticker, Dr. John and Lumpkin, Dr. Susan. *Dangerous Animals.* Austrailia: US Weldon Owen Inc., 1995.

Do you Remember?

Do you remember?
Grandma Hannah would be looking out the
window,
From her comfy big chair,
Watching us kids play in her yard outside,
Wishing she was out there.

Yes, I remember,
She'd call for us to come in and visit,
She loved to sit and talk,
After a few short hours we headed home,
It was only a short walk.

Do you remember?
The first time we tried to make an Angel Food
Cake,
We thought we would be so cool,
But somehow we forgot about it,
When we ran outside to jump in the pool.

Yes, I remember,
It was suppose to be a surprise,
But we made a mess all over the kitchen floor,
And when we remembered to check the cake,
A cloud of black smoke came out of the oven
door.

Do you remember?
Walking through the field to reach the creek,
Where we would spend the day,
Enjoying the peace and quite,
Wondering what the tall trees would say.

Yes, I remember,
Going down there to fish,
Sitting in the tall grass and feeling the warm
sun,
That was our lazy days of summer,
And it sure was fun!

Accept Others!

A poem by
Jessica Lee

"Hey up there?" said Ivy.
"Your tall and thin.
If there'd be a bean pole contest,
I'm sure you'd win!"

"Hey down there? I'm Eb.
Do you play sports at all?
You could easily be mistaken
For a soccer ball!"

Those two certainly can't be friends.
How people would talk, oh my!
Their weight and height would be
an issue,
People would laugh as they walked by!

Ivy smiled, "I could lose some weight,
and become full of charm.
My dad is very rich,
But I'm sure he wouldn't bet
the farm!"

"Yeah," said Eb, "And I could gain
some weight.
I'll eat and eat, 24 hours a day,
Though I don't think I could afford to,
My parents don't get much for pay."

"Maybe," sighed Ivy,
"Nobody would notice,
How different we really are.
Oh, but to cross that finish line,
Seems way to far."

But for them to be friends,
How would their parents take
the news?
They wouldn't understand if
they said,
Please take a walk in their shoes.

"If I'd bring you home today,
I know for sure one thing,
My parents disapproval and
screaming,
Would make my ears ring!"

"Maybe if we could change our race,
Even if just for a day,
We might get to hear,
Sure, that girl can come over
and play!"

"Now let's scrub that black color off.
On your hands, neck and nose,
And don't forget the cracks,
Between your fingers and your toes!"

"It didn't come off, Ivy!
That didn't work so well.
Let's paint you,
Black suits you just swell."

"But what's this?
It's wearing off fast.
Now the white shows through,
I knew it wouldn't last!"

Ivy cried, "Why should we have to
change ourselves?
It's just not worth the fight.
God made everyone different,
And that should make it right!"

The girls saw each other that year
in school,
But hardly any words to each other,
did they say.
Until their 6th grade graduation,
Which was held the second week
in May.

Everyone enjoyed the celebration.
Their parents talked
while having punch.
But you can't imagine,
Eb and Ivy's surprise,
When they heard them say,
"Let's do lunch!"

Your Own Personal Journal

This is a special section just for you.

It's a place for you to write down some exciting things that have gone on in your life.

When your finished with the Journal, share what you have written, with others.

You will be amazed at how much fun it is to write about yourself and have others listen to you as you tell them about some of the special things in your life.

Your Personal Journal

1. Write a short story about a couple of your best friends.

_____
_____
_____
_____
_____
_____
_____
_____
_____
_____
_____
_____
_____
_____
_____
_____
_____
_____

2. Write a short story about one of the best birthday parties you have ever been to.

_____

_____

_____

_____

_____

_____

_____

_____

_____

_____

_____

_____

_____

_____

_____

_____

_____

3. Write a short story about your
favorite animal.

_____

_____

_____

_____

_____

_____

_____

_____

_____

_____

_____

_____

_____

_____

_____

_____

_____

4. What is the funniest thing that has
   ever happened to you?

_____

_____

_____

_____

_____

_____

_____

_____

_____

_____

_____

_____

_____

_____

_____

_____

_____

_____

_____

5. What is the scariest thing that has ever happened to you?

_____

_____

_____

_____

_____

_____

_____

_____

_____

_____

_____

_____

_____

_____

_____

_____

_____

_____

_____